ANIMALS
ANIMALS

PENGUINS

BY JUDITH JANGO-COHEN

BENCHMARK BOOKS

MARSHALL CAVENDISH
NEW YORK

Series Consultant:
James Doherty, General Curator
The Bronx Zoo, New York

Benchmark Books
Marshall Cavendish Corporation
99 White Plains Road
Tarrytown, NY 10591–9001
Website: www.marshallcavendish.com

Library of Congress Cataloging–in–Publication Data
Jango–Cohen, Judith.
Penguins / by Judith Jango–Cohen.
p. cm. – (Animals, animals)
ISBN 0–7614–1260–3
1. Penguins–Juvenile literature. [1. Penguins.] I. Title. II. Series.

QL696.S473 J36 2001   598.47–dc21   00–049812

Photo research by Anne Burns Images

Cover photo: © Kevin Schafer

The photographs in this book are used by permission and through the courtesy of: *Animals Animals:* G. L. Kooyman, 6, 21; D. Ikenberry, 10; Eastcott/Momatiuk, 14 (top left); Maresa Pryor, 14 (top right); John Gerlach, 14 (bottom left); Johnny Johnson, 14 (bottom right), 19 (left); K. Westerkov, 15 (top); Mark A. Chappell, 28; Gerard Lacz, 34; Michael Bisceglie, 40. *Kevin Schafer:* 4, 8, 12, 12 (inset), 17 (inset), 19 (right), 24, 28, 43. *Peter Arnold, Inc.:* Kevin Schafer, 15 (middle), 17, 22, 23, 29, 38; Roland Seitre, 33. *Wolfgang Kaehler:* 26, 30, 36.

Printed in Hong Kong

1 3 5 6 4 2

CONTENTS

1
INTRODUCING PENGUINS

Five hundred years ago, curious explorers on tall sailing ships stared at a strange creature. It leapt from the sea and then slipped back in, weaving in and out of the water. Tiny furlike feathers coated its sleek body, which was fitted with two stiff flippers. What kind of bizarre beast was this, the sailors wondered—a flippered bird . . . or a feathered fish?

These sailors had seen their first penguin. Penguins are birds. They lay eggs and have feathers. But in the bird world penguins are oddballs. They cannot fly. Beneath the waves, though,

IN 1578, AN EXPLORER DESCRIBED PENGUINS LIKE THESE ADÉLIES AS WALKING "SO UPRIGHT THAT A FAR-OFF MAN WOULD TAKE THEM TO BE LITTLE CHILDREN."

5

SLEEK, STREAMLINED BODIES HELP THESE EMPEROR PENGUINS STREAK THROUGH THE WATER AS FAST AS SEALS.

they swerve and swoop like swallows through clouds of shimmering fish. Clearly, they are built for the sea—not for the sky.

While most birds are high fliers, penguins are deep divers. Hollow, air-filled bones may be perfect for parrots and pigeons, but not for penguins. Their bones are solid, heavy enough to help them stay submerged while they search for food and sturdy enough not to break under the heavy water pressure.

How do penguins push themselves through the heavy water? Long, floppy wings would not work well, but a penguin's short, flat flippers are just right. Like a paddle, their flippers are stiff–they do not bend at the wrist and elbow, which is why penguins cannot fold up their flippers. Even the feathers on their flippers are short and stiff. Long, flexible feathers would slow these divers down.

Like human divers, penguins have a special suit to keep them warm. What is this diving suit made of? Feathers! Penguin feathers are stubby, stiff, and close together. A dozen feathers or more are crammed into an area the size of your fingernail. Packed together, these feathers overlap to seal out wind and water. And being short and stiff, they are not easily ruffled by a cold breeze.

Besides this dense suit penguins have three other ways to *insulate*, or protect, themselves from the cold.

YELLOW-EYED PENGUINS HELP EACH OTHER TO PREEN THOSE HARD-TO-REACH PLACES.

They coat their feathers with waterproof oil made by a gland near their tails. When penguins *preen*, they work the oil in with their beaks and flippers. Second, downy tufts at the base of each feather trap the heat from their bodies. *Blubber*, a fatty layer below their skin, helps too.

Penguins need to bundle up because they feed only in the chilly, food–filled seas in the southern half of the world, around *Antarctica*. They live wherever the cold Antarctic waters flow, as far north as the equator.

8

PENGUIN HABITAT

Pacific Ocean

GALÁPAGOS ISLANDS

South America

equator

SOUTH AMERICA

AFRICA

SOUTH POLE ANTARCTICA

NEW ZEALAND

AUSTRALIA

PENGUINS CAN BE FOUND ANYWHERE IN THE SOUTHERN HEMISPHERE WHERE THERE ARE COLD OCEAN CURRENTS. THE HIGHLIGHTED AREAS INDICATE THE COASTAL REGIONS THAT PENGUINS INHABIT. THE MOST NORTHERLY PENGUINS ARE FOUND ON THE EQUATOR IN THE GALÁPAGOS ISLANDS.

Some of these icy waters sweep past hot, steamy lands. There are penguins that come ashore onto hardened lava islands near the equator. Others shuffle onto sandy deserts on the shores of South America. Although all penguins swim in chilly waters, they live on land in many different types of environments, or *habitats*.

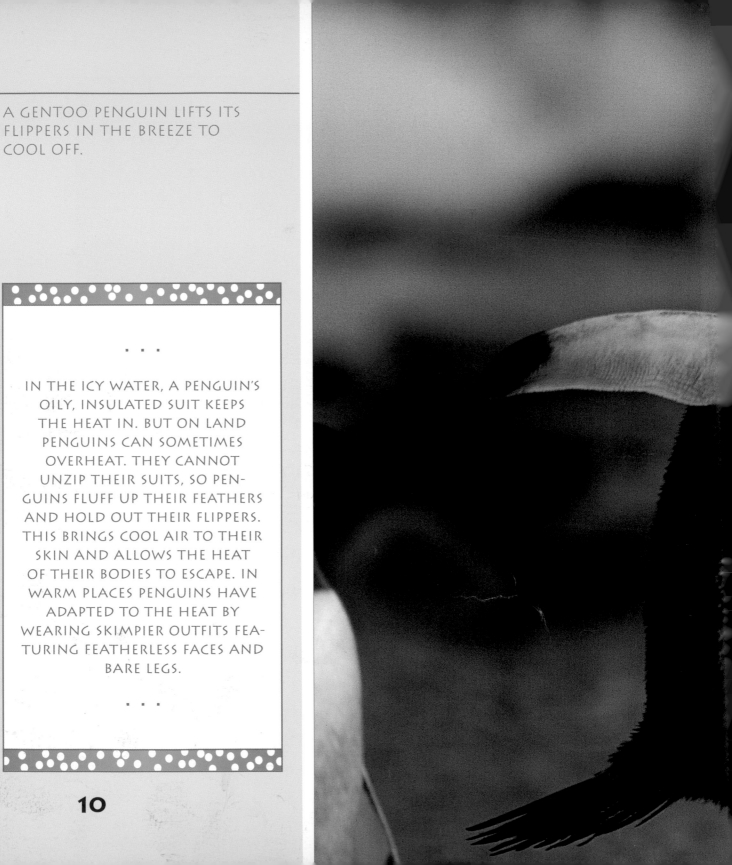

A GENTOO PENGUIN LIFTS ITS
FLIPPERS IN THE BREEZE TO
COOL OFF.

. . .

IN THE ICY WATER, A PENGUIN'S
OILY, INSULATED SUIT KEEPS
THE HEAT IN. BUT ON LAND
PENGUINS CAN SOMETIMES
OVERHEAT. THEY CANNOT
UNZIP THEIR SUITS, SO PEN-
GUINS FLUFF UP THEIR FEATHERS
AND HOLD OUT THEIR FLIPPERS.
THIS BRINGS COOL AIR TO THEIR
SKIN AND ALLOWS THE HEAT
OF THEIR BODIES TO ESCAPE. IN
WARM PLACES PENGUINS HAVE
ADAPTED TO THE HEAT BY
WEARING SKIMPIER OUTFITS FEA-
TURING FEATHERLESS FACES AND
BARE LEGS.

. . .

HARDY ADÉLIE PENGUINS MAKE THEIR WAY TO THE TOP OF AN ICEBERG.

(OPPOSITE) ROYAL PENGUINS LAND ON SNOW-FREE MACQUARIE ISLAND, LOCATED BETWEEN SOUTHERN AUSTRALIA AND ANTARCTICA.

A popular penguin joke claims that there are only two kinds of penguins: the black ones waddling away from you, and the white ones coming toward you. Actually, there are eighteen types, or *species*, of penguins. Some are only black and white, but others flash plumes or patches of orange, red, or pink. Some penguins' legs and faces are covered with feathers, while on others these places are bare. Penguins differ in size too, from the burly emperor to the tiny little blue.

All penguins are alike in basic ways because they need to keep warm in cold water. But they differ because each species has had to *adapt* to a different kind of habitat on land.

PENGUIN SPECIES

Six of the eighteen existing species of penguins are shown below along with the average height and weight of an adult.

LITTLE BLUE,
OR FAIRY
16 INCHES
(40 CM)
2.2 POUNDS
(1 KG)

GALAPAGOS
20 INCHES
(53 CM)
5.5 POUNDS
(2.5 KG)

ROCKHOPPER
22.5 INCHES
(58 CM)
7.5 POUNDS
(3.4 KG)

ADÉLIE
27.5 INCHES
(70 CM)
8.5 POUNDS
(4 KG)

YELLOW-EYED
29 INCHES
(75 CM)
13 POUNDS
(6 KG)

EMPEROR
51 INCHES
(130 CM)
83.5 POUNDS
(38 KG)

THIS IS A PENGUIN SKELETON. NOTE THE
BROAD, FLAT BONES OF THE WINGS.
THESE FORM THE PADDLELIKE FLIPPERS
THAT HELP MAKE PENGUINS SUCH GOOD
SWIMMERS. THE LEGS ARE SET FAR BACK
ON THE BODY, WHICH CAUSES PENGUINS
TO STAND UPRIGHT WHEN ON LAND.

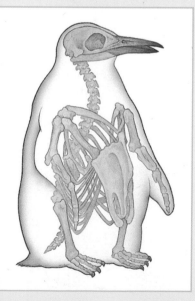

2
MAKING A LANDING

All winter, penguins are out at sea filling up with food. But when spring warms the air, they travel back to shore—back to the land, where their life began.

Along the Falkland Islands, near South America, waves bash against the ancient cliffs. In the swirling foam little rockhopper penguins bob around, trying to reach land. They are tossed by the pounding surf but, after many attempts, finally leap ashore. Now the rock-hoppers have yet another challenge. Their nesting sites are 300 feet (92 m) straight up. As their name suggests, they will reach the cliff top by hopping!

Rockhoppers' ankles are extra strong and their toe-nails are long—useful tools for gripping slippery stone. With their heads forward, flippers back, and two pink feet held together, they bounce up the narrow cliff trail, strewn with crumbling boulders. The trail is scarred with grooves scratched out by troops of rockhoppers, over hundreds of years.

SLIPPERY STONES DON'T STOP THESE ROCKHOPPER
PENGUINS FROM CLIMBING ASHORE.

(LEFT) ROCKHOPPERS USE THEIR LONG TOENAILS AND
STRONG BEAKS TO GRIP THE CLIFFS AS THEY CLIMB
TO THEIR NESTS.

Finally the rockhoppers reach the summit. They have conquered the cliff and are back in their summer home. Throughout the southern seas, male penguins, who usually return first, are staking out nesting sites. Fights flare up over the best spots. Some penguins chase and stab at each other with bloodied beaks. Others hold flipper–slapping matches. After the brawl, the winner tips back his head, flaps his flippers, and sings in victory.

When the females arrive, most return to their old partners. Others choose a new mate. How do they decide? Females like males with low voices. The deeper the vocal tone and the bulkier the body, the better he probably is at fishing. Females also select mates with brightly colored feathers—a sign of good health. After the match is made, the partners sing a duet. Then they may sway and bow in a mating dance.

When the singing and dancing are over, the nest–building begins. Penguins in hot places search out cool *burrows*, shady bushes, and caves to avoid overheating their eggs. In cold areas penguins build mounds to raise their eggs off the chilly ground and to prevent melting snow from flooding the nests.

THE BRIGHT ORANGE PATCHES
ABOVE MALE KING PENGUINS' EARS
HELP THEM TO ATTRACT MATES.

THIS YELLOW-EYED PENGUIN
HAS FOUND A SAFE NESTING
PLACE UNDER THE ROOTS OF
A FALLEN TREE.

Penguins build their nests with grass, stones, sea-weed, and bones—whatever they can find. Scientists have even reported seeing penguins grab a glass, a spoon, and half a chocolate bar from their camp. Penguins also swipe nesting material from neighbors when they are not looking.

ADÉLIE PENGUIN EGGS REST IN STONE NESTS, OUT OF REACH OF THE MELTING SNOW.

AN EMPEROR PENGUIN ROCKETS FROM THE SEA ONTO THE SHORE
IN ANTARCTICA.

After laying her eggs, the female leaves the nesting site. She needs to eat to rebuild her strength. The male stays and protects the eggs. He too will go fishing, but only when his mate returns. Penguins share guard duty for several weeks, even when storms splatter them with mud or bury them in snow.

All penguins take nest-sitting seriously, but when it comes to parenting, emperor penguins win the prize. Every autumn, while other penguins are still feasting at sea, emperors streak toward the frozen Antarctic. They make a landing on the slick ice by leaping from

21

SOMETIMES SLIDING IS THE BEST WAY FOR EMPEROR PENGUINS TO TRAVEL ON SNOWY SLOPES.

the water and plopping onto their plump, blubbery tummies.

To reach safe mating grounds, where ice will not melt and float away in the spring, they sometimes must journey over one hundred miles (160 km). Waddling won't do, so they flop onto their bellies and slide, pushing with their feet and flippers.

Emperors do not try to build nests on the frozen ground. They cradle their eggs on their feet and cover them with their feathery belly flap. Soon the females leave to eat, and the males huddle together for two months, without food, through brutal cold and

THE ONLY WARM
SPOT FOR THIS
EMPEROR PENGUIN
EGG IS BETWEEN
ITS PARENT'S
BELLY AND FEET.

darkness. (In Antarctica the sun will not rise until spring.) When the females return, they will find nestled on their partner's feet, not an egg—but a hungry chick.

23

THIS GROUP OF EMPEROR
PENGUINS IS ON A LONG
JOURNEY BACK TO ITS
MATING GROUNDS.

3
FAMILY LIFE

Being born is not easy for a penguin chick. After struggling for a day, it finally tumbles out of its shell—tired, wet, and skinny. Its eyes are sealed shut, but its beak is not. Stubborn squeaks tell its parents, "I want to eat!"

Penguin parents feed their chicks a slimy, pre-digested, baby food which they cough up when the chicks peck at their beaks. At first mealtime is a mushy mess. But chicks quickly learn to eat neatly by poking their heads right inside their parents' throats.

Chicks who have not learned this trick may lose their lunch to clever gulls. These birds dash toward a feeding chick to distract it. Then they grab the snack that splatters to the ground. Gulls also dine on unguarded eggs and on dead chicks.

ONCE THEY GROW TOO BIG TO SNUGGLE UP WITH THEIR PARENTS, EMPEROR CHICKS HUDDLE TOGETHER IN GROUPS CALLED CRÈCHES TO KEEP WARM.

Another bird that patrols penguin areas is the sharp-clawed skua. Skuas team up to tease nesting penguins. One pulls a penguin's tail, and when the penguin turns around, the other skua snatches the egg or chick. Depending upon where they nest, the penguins may face other hunters, or *predators*, such as snakes, crabs, foxes, ferrets, and rats.

To guard against these predators, one parent stays at the nest while the other goes for food. But after a few weeks the chicks' appetites have grown so much that usually both parents must go fishing together. What happens to the chicks? Unless they can hide in burrows, chicks clump together into groups called *crèches*. These clusters keep them warm, and predators are not as quick to attack a chick in a crowd.

28

KING PENGUIN CHICKS
LOOK SO DIFFERENT
FROM THE ADULTS
THAT PEOPLE USED TO
THINK THEY WERE A
SEPARATE SPECIES.

AS THIS KING PENGUIN MOLTS, NEW FEATHERS GROW IN AND THE OLD ONES ARE PUSHED OUT.

How long do penguins live? Those who survive predators, winter fasting, and the harsh conditions of the Antarctic, can live to be 15 to 20 years old.

Crèches may contain a few dozen chicks or as many as a thousand. Some chicks may be part of a *colony*, or group, of more than one million penguins! How do chicks find their parents in this mob? When parents return, they call their chicks to dinner. Recognizing their voices, the chicks waddle to them. If a strange chick comes calling, the adults send it away with a peck or a slap of their flipper.

Sometimes parents make chicks chase them for their meal. This may prepare them for their difficult hunting days ahead. But before they can fish for them-selves, chicks must be outfitted properly. They must *molt*, or shed, their fluffy *down*. Only when their slick, waterproof gear grows in can they head out to sea.

The late summer water is so ripe with food even clumsy young penguins can catch a bite. It also helps that most of the adults, who are practiced hunters, are not around. They are molting on shore, replacing their worn feathers with sturdy new ones. But finding food is just one of a young penguin's problems. Only about half of them will survive their first few months at sea.

4
SEA WORLD

Young Adélie penguins, with wisps of down still cling-ing to their new feathers, line up on a ledge. Suddenly, a rolling wall of water washes them into the sea. Although this is their first dip in the surf, they know how to swim. One curious young penguin paddles over to a dark lump floating nearby. The lump has two eyes, a nose, and, as the penguin finds out too late, large toothy jaws. For leopard seals, young penguins are easy-to-get snacks. But to catch adult penguins, leopard seals must use different tricks. Sometimes they swim beneath penguins that are walking on thin ice. Then they bash through the ice and grab the bird. Other times, they wait near high, icy ledges where penguins have trouble landing. When the penguins get tired, the leopard seals move in.

THESE ADÉLIE PENGUINS ARE AS GRACEFUL AS OLYMPIC DIVERS.

Penguins' white fronts and black backs provide camouflage in the water. Their black backs can make it difficult to see them from above against the dark seas. Their white fronts may make them hard to recognize from below, against the light surface. This creates a challenge for predators such as seals, sharks, and killer whales when they hunt for penguins.

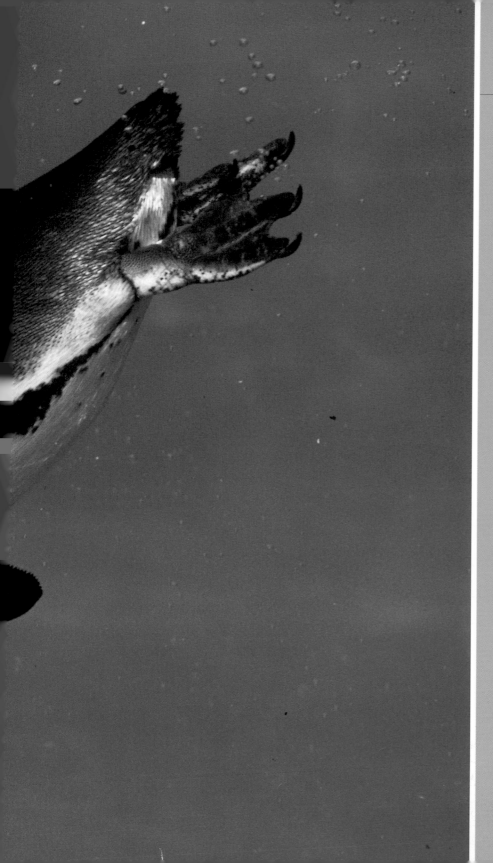

A GALÁPAGOS PENGUIN
MOVES SWIFTLY TO CATCH
ITS DINNER.

Other animals that enjoy penguin meat are sharks, sea lions, and killer whales. But penguins have ways to outwit these predators. They only hunt in groups because dozens of watchful eyes are better than two. And when a predator races after them, they leap out of the water, quickly switching direction when they dive back in.

Penguins cannot avoid these dangerous encounters because they must go fishing for their own food. Penguins, which are predators too, hunt squid, shrimp–like *krill*, and fish.

How do hungry penguins hang onto their slippery *prey*? Their tools include a sharp beak and pointy spines that line their mouth and tongue. When penguins catch a fish they turn it around in their beak and swallow it head first. This prevents the fins from fanning out and getting caught in their throat. The pointy spines grip the fish and keep it from changing direction half-way down.

Penguins must work hard to find their dinner. Sometimes they fish for twelve to fifteen hours a day, making three or four hundred dives. These dives may be as deep as 150 feet (45 m). Penguins can go even deeper though. The emperor has been recorded at depths of over 1,300 feet (400 m). That is as deep as 130 ten-foot swimming pools!

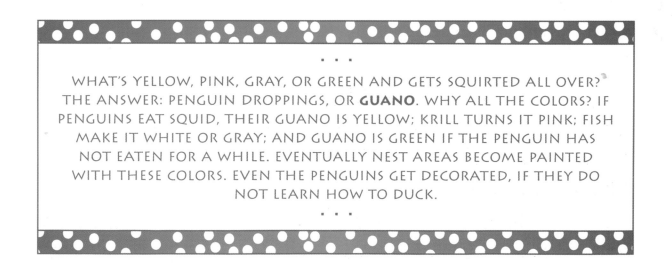

. . .

WHAT'S YELLOW, PINK, GRAY, OR GREEN AND GETS SQUIRTED ALL OVER? THE ANSWER: PENGUIN DROPPINGS, OR **GUANO**. WHY ALL THE COLORS? IF PENGUINS EAT SQUID, THEIR GUANO IS YELLOW; KRILL TURNS IT PINK; FISH MAKE IT WHITE OR GRAY; AND GUANO IS GREEN IF THE PENGUIN HAS NOT EATEN FOR A WHILE. EVENTUALLY NEST AREAS BECOME PAINTED WITH THESE COLORS. EVEN THE PENGUINS GET DECORATED, IF THEY DO NOT LEARN HOW TO DUCK.

. . .

5

PENGUINS AND PEOPLE

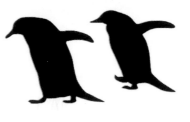

Early sailors may not have known what penguins were, but they knew they could eat them. They didn't much like the taste, but they stocked up on penguin meat for use on their long ocean voyages. Sailors also ate penguin eggs, sometimes gathering thousands from one colony. In the 1800s, people killed penguins for their blubber, which they boiled to make oil.

Penguins are no longer killed in this way, but they face other

THESE EMPEROR PENGUINS WILL HAVE TO MAKE WAY FOR AN APPROACHING RUSSIAN ICEBREAKER.

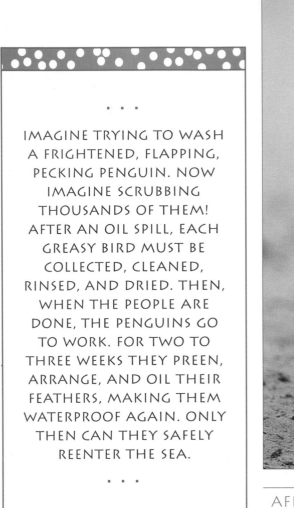

. . .

IMAGINE TRYING TO WASH A FRIGHTENED, FLAPPING, PECKING PENGUIN. NOW IMAGINE SCRUBBING THOUSANDS OF THEM! AFTER AN OIL SPILL, EACH GREASY BIRD MUST BE COLLECTED, CLEANED, RINSED, AND DRIED. THEN, WHEN THE PEOPLE ARE DONE, THE PENGUINS GO TO WORK. FOR TWO TO THREE WEEKS THEY PREEN, ARRANGE, AND OIL THEIR FEATHERS, MAKING THEM WATERPROOF AGAIN. ONLY THEN CAN THEY SAFELY REENTER THE SEA.

. . .

AFRICAN PENGUINS ARE PLAGUED BY OIL SPILLS BECAUSE THEY LIVE CLOSE TO BUSY SHIPPING LANES.

dangers because of threats to their habitat. When people clear land for homes and farms, they may be destroying penguin homes. Also, domestic animals that humans bring in, like cats, dogs, and cattle, may attack penguins or trample their nests.

40

People are affecting penguins at sea too. The growing human population needs increasing amounts of fish, squid, and krill—all foods that penguins eat. In addition, fishing nets can trap and kill penguins. Huge tankers are another threat because they have been known to spill oil. Those penguins that will not enter the polluted water may starve. Those that do dive in become coated with oil. Then they are poisoned or die of cold because their feathers can no longer insulate them.

Although some people create problems for penguins, others are trying to find solutions. In some places they are replacing plants to provide nesting sites. They are also setting aside areas where penguins will be protected. And after tanker spills, volunteers rush to rescue oil-covered birds. Scientists gather every two years at the International Penguin Conference to share the new things they have learned about penguins, and to discuss ways to keep them safe.

Penguins have people appeal. We think they are cute, tottering around in stylish black and white. But penguins are also beautiful, sliding through the sea, trailing ribbons of bubbles. They are tough birds, deep divers, and hardy rock climbers. They outsmart sea lions and outlast blasting blizzards—while balancing an egg on their feet! Perhaps more than any bird in the world, penguins have the power to amuse, amaze, and inspire us.

PENGUIN EXPERTS HOPE THAT THE PENGUIN'S "CUTENESS FACTOR" WILL TRANSLATE INTO STRENGTHENED PROTECTION EFFORTS. THE MORE WE LEARN ABOUT THE REMARKABLE WORLD OF PENGUINS, THE MORE LIKELY WE ARE TO HELP KEEP THEM SAFE.

43

adapt: to change in ways that help a living thing to survive

Antarctica: the continent that surrounds the South Pole.

blubber: a layer of fat below a penguin's skin that may be an inch (2.5 cm) thick. It helps insulate the penguin, but is mainly used for energy storage.

burrow: holes that penguins dig with their beaks and feet in the ground, grass, and even in dried layers of guano, to be used as nests.

camouflage: colors and patterns on an animal that hide its true shape.

colony: a group of nesting penguins made up of a few, or of more than a million, birds

crèche: a group of penguin chicks that gather together for warmth and protection

down: a covering of soft, fluffy feathers

equator: an imaginary line around the earth that lies halfway between the North and South poles

guano: seabird or bat droppings

habitat: the place where a plant or animal lives

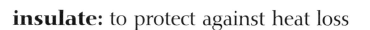

insulate: to protect against heat loss

krill: shrimplike animals that may swarm in the millions, some-times turning the surface of the sea red

molt: to lose old feathers and grow new ones. Birds usually molt once a year.

predator: an animal that hunts and eats other animals

preen: to clean, arrange, and oil the feathers

prey: an animal that is hunted and eaten by another

species: a single kind of plant or animal

BOOKS

Dewey, Jennifer Owings. *Birds of Antarctica: The Adélie Penguin.* Boston: Little, Brown, 1989.

Kalman, Bobbie. *Penguins.* New York: Crabtree Publishing Company, 1995.

Lynch, Wayne. *Penguins!* Toronto, Ontario: Firefly Books, 1999.

Ollason, Robert. *Penguin Parade.* Minneapolis: Lerner Publications, 1995.

Patent, Dorothy Hinshaw. *Looking at Penguins.* New York: Holiday House, 1993.

Resnick, Jane. *Penguins.* Chicago: Kidsbooks, 1997.

Somme, Lauritz and Sybille Kalas. *The Penguin Family Book.* Saxonville, MA: Picture Book Studio, 1988.

Switzer, Merebeth. *Penguins.* Danbury, CT: Grolier Educational Corporation, 1990.

VIDEOS

Emperors of Antarctica. Discovery Productions, 1992.

Penguins: Creatures of the Sea. Thirteen/WNET, 1995.

Penguin World. Smithsonian Institution, 1992.

WEBSITES

Adélie and Emperor Penguin Pictures and Calls
http:// sung3.ifsi.rm.cnr.it/~dargaud/Antarctica/Penguins.html

Adélie Penguin
http:// expage.com/page/adeliepenguin

Emperor Penguins
http:// www.geocities.com/RainForest/Canopy/7897/penguins.html

New Zealand Penguins
http://www.penguin.net.nz

Penguins, Penguins, Penguins
http://members.aol.com/Avena/penguins.html

Pete and Barb's Penguin Pages
http://ourworld.compuserve.com/homepages/Peter_and_Barbara_Barham/
pengies.htm

Penguin exhibit at the Central Park Wildlife Center, New York
http://www.earthcam.com/usa/newyork/cpzoo/

WHERE TO SEE PENGUINS IN ZOOS

Many zoos have penguin exhibits that include species found in South American and African coastal waters. These penguins do not require the cold air temperatures that Antarctic species need. Here is a list of some of the biggest and best penguin exhibits in the United States and Canada.

USA

BALTIMORE ZOO, MARYLAND
CENTRAL PARK ZOO, NEW YORK CITY
HENRY DOORLY ZOO, OMAHA
NEW YORK AQUARIUM, BROOKLYN, NEW YORK
SAN FRANCISCO ZOO, CALIFORNIA

SEAWORLD, SAN ANTONIO, TEXAS
SEAWORLD, SAN DIEGO, CALIFORNIA
SHEDD AQUARIUM, CHICAGO, ILLINOIS

CANADA

BIODOME, MONTREAL

ABOUT THE AUTHOR

Judith Jango–Cohen taught science for ten years before she started writing books. She learns about the animals she writes about by exploring national parks. On her travels Judith takes along her husband, Eliot, and her two children, Jennifer and Steven. Although she enjoys writing about animals, her family does not have any pets. Her children however, hope to change that.

INDEX

Page numbers in **boldface** are illustrations.